FAMILIES AROUND THE WORLD

A family from CHINA

Julia Waterlow

WAYLAND

FAMILIES AROUND THE WORLD

A family from **BOSNIA**

A family from **BRAZIL**

A family from **CHINA**

A family from **ETHIOPIA**

A family from **GERMANY**

A family from **GUATEMALA**

A family from **IRAQ**

A family from **JAPAN**

A family from **SOUTH AFRICA**

A family from **VIETNAM**

The family featured in this book is an average Chinese family. The Wus have been chosen because they are typical of the majority of Chinese families in terms of income, housing, number of children and lifestyle.

Cover: The Wu family outside their home with all their possessions.
Title page: Jian Chun and Rong wash clothes outside their home.
Contents page: Two women cycle to work.

Series editor: Katie Orchard
Book editor: Alison Cooper
Designer: Tim Mayer
Production controller: Carol Titchener

Picture Acknowledgements: All the photographs in this book were taken by Leong Ka Tai. The photographs were supplied by Material World/Impact Photos and were first published in 1994 by Sierra Club Books in *Material World: A Global Family Portrait* © Copyright Peter Menzel/Material World. The map artwork on page 4 was produced by Peter Bull.

First published in 1998 by Wayland Publishers Limited
61 Western Road, Hove
East Sussex, BN3 1JD, England

© Copyright 1998 Wayland Publishers Limited

Find Wayland on the Internet at http://www.wayland.co.uk

Typeset by Mayer Media
Printed and bound in Italy by G. Canale & C.S.p.A., Turin.

British Library Cataloguing in Publication Data

Waterlow, Julia
    A family from China. – (Families around the world)
    1. Family – China – Juvenile literature
    2. China – Social life and customs – Juvenile literature
    I. Title
306.8'5'0951

ISBN 0 7502 1999 8

Contents

Introduction

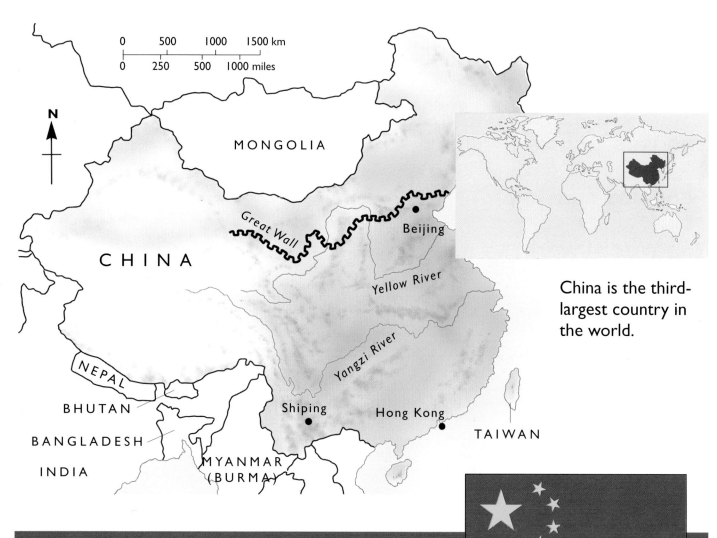

China is the third-largest country in the world.

CHINA

Capital city:	Beijing
Size:	9,597,000 square kilometres
Number of people:	1,251,000,000
Language:	Mainly Mandarin Chinese
People:	93 per cent are Chinese.
Religion:	Not many Chinese are religious. Some are Buddhists. A few people are Muslims or Christians.
Currency:	Yuan

THE WU FAMILY

Size of household:	9 people
Size of home:	110 square metres
Work week:	60 hours at busy times of year (adults)
Most valued possessions:	Ba Jiu: His television Dong: His bicycle
Family income:	US$3,300 each year

The Wu family is an ordinary Chinese family. They have put everything that they own outside their home so that this photograph could be taken.

Meet the Wu family

1 Ba Jiu, father, 59
2 Yu Xian (you say 'Yoo She-en'), mother, 57
3 Wen De, elder son, 30
4 Jian Chun ('Jee-en Choon'), his wife, 28
5 Dong, their son, 8
6 Xi ('Shee'), their daughter, 3
7 Wen Bin, second son, 25
8 Rong, his wife, 25
9 Xue ('Shway'), their daughter, 3

A CROWDED COUNTRY

More people live in China than in any other country in the world. Because China is becoming very crowded, most families are only allowed to have one child. In the countryside, families are allowed to have two children.

Ba Jiu and Yu Xian live with their sons, who are grown up and have families of their own. Their elder son, Wen De, has a wife and two children. Their younger son, Wen Bin, is also married. He has one daughter. Ba Jiu and Yu Xian are very happy to have their children and grandchildren living with them, and everyone in the family gets on well.

'We are allowed to have two children. We hope our second child will be a boy.' *Rong.*

The Wus' house

The Wus' house is a traditional Chinese house. It has curved roofs and is built around a courtyard. In front of the house there is a big fish pond.

TOWN AND COUNTRY

Most people in China still live in towns or villages in the countryside. They usually have more space in their houses than the Chinese who live in cities. China's cities are very crowded. Many people live in tiny flats, with just one or two rooms.

A Country Home

The Wus are a family of farmers who live in southern China. Their house is in the countryside. It takes them fifteen minutes to walk to the nearest village, which is called Shiping.

Inside the Wus' house, there is a living room, a kitchen and three bedrooms. There are several store rooms as well. Here, the Wus keep tools, food, bits of wood and even old newspapers and boxes. Ba Jiu doesn't like to throw useful things away. Outside, there is also a sheltered area, where the Wus keep their pigs.

'I'm used to doing the washing by hand, but it would be nice to have a washing machine.' *Jian Chun.*

There is no tap inside the house, so the family collects water every day from a tap nearby. Rong and Jian Chun usually do the washing in a pool at the side of the house.

'We like to watch television together in the evenings.' *Ba Jiu*.

Old and New

Ba Jiu and Yu Xian like the old furniture in the living room. The rest of the family prefers modern furniture, so Wen De and Wen Bin have bought some new chairs. One thing that everyone likes is the colour television. It is in the middle of the room so that everyone can watch it easily.

Hot Summers

In summer it gets very hot, so the Wus have electric fans in each room. When it gets too warm, they switch on the fans to keep the rooms cool.
The family all have net curtains around their beds. They pull the curtains round at night so that mosquitoes can't bite them while they are asleep. There are always lots of mosquitoes in the summer.

Dong keeps his toys in a cupboard in his parents' bedroom.

Food and cooking

The Wus store dried and pickled food in jars and baskets.

RICE AND NOODLES

The Chinese eat either rice or noodles with their meals. People in southern China mostly eat rice, and people in northern China mostly eat noodles. Rice grows best in the south, where the weather is warmer and wetter.

Storing Food

The Wus grow most of their food themselves. They dry or pickle food such as cabbage, beans and fish, and put it in big jars. This way, they can keep the food for several months and it will still be good to eat.

Rice With Everything

The Wus eat rice with every meal. For breakfast they have a kind of sticky rice, and the children drink soya milk, which is made from a type of bean. For lunch and supper everyone eats rice with vegetables. Sometimes, the family has fish too. They don't eat meat very often because it is too expensive.

Wen De spoons his breakfast into a small bowl. The Wus eat their food with chopsticks.

Fast Food

Yu Xian likes to prepare the food for special meals, when the whole family eats together. First, she chops the food up into small pieces. This is so that the food cooks quickly and she doesn't have to use too much fuel. She fries or boils most of the food in a big wok. Yu Xian saves time by using an electric steamer to cook the rice.

This big pan is called a wok. Yu Xian is making soup in it.

'I prepare the food for my family sometimes. They all say I'm a great cook!' *Wen De*.

The Wus at work

The Wus grow vegetables and keep fish. Wen Bin wears plastic overalls so that he can wade into the pond to catch the fish.

WORKERS IN CHINA

In China, most women work, as well as looking after their families. Many Chinese people still work in the countryside as farmers. Often, young people move to the cities, where they hope they will find better-paid jobs.

Fishing Folk

The pond in front of the Wus' house is full of fish. The Wus share the pond with their neighbours. Wen De and Wen Bin feed the fish until they are big enough to eat. Then they catch and sell them.

16

'We can make a lot of money from our fish, so we have to make sure they are well fed.' *Wen Bin*.

Looking after fish is hard work. Every few days, Wen De and Wen Bin take their boat to Jade Dragon Lake, not far from their house. Here, they collect weed which the fish like to eat. The fish are quite valuable, so the Wus and their neighbours take turns to guard the pond at night. Otherwise, thieves might come and steal the fish. The Wus have been lucky – no one has stolen any fish yet.

Wen De and Wen Bin collect weed from Jade Dragon Lake.

Everyday Work

The Wus always have plenty of jobs to do. Wen De and Wen Bin look after the fish. Rong and Jian Chun take care of the pigs. They do the housework, such as washing and cleaning, as well. Yu Xian and Ba Jiu help by looking after their grandchildren, Xi and Xue, while everyone else is busy.

The Wus have planted some orange trees. Wen De is starting to pick the ripe fruit.

The Wus grow all kinds of vegetables to sell at the market. Their onions and cabbages are especially good. Everyone helps in the fields, planting, watering, hoeing and picking. They have to do all the work by hand.

Busy Times

Yu Xian and Ba Jiu carry their vegetables to market in bamboo baskets.

The Wus are very busy at certain times of the year. The busiest times are when the fish are ready for market, and when the vegetables and rice have to be planted and harvested. Then, everyone works from sunrise to sunset. Even Dong, who is only eight, has to help.

Sunday is market day in Shiping. Yu Xian and Ba Jiu set off early to take the vegetables to the market. Ba Jiu always sells the vegetables himself.

'People like to buy vegetables from me. I must have an honest face!' *Ba Jiu.*

School and play

Wen De's son, Dong, goes to the local school in Shiping.

There is no alphabet in Chinese. Instead, each word is written as a 'character', like the ones on the wall in the picture at the top of page 23. Chinese children have to learn thousands of characters by heart when they are learning to read and write.

Off To School

It is still dark when Dong gets up to go to school. After a quick breakfast, he dashes off to reach his school in Shiping by half-past seven. He is usually late, and has to run most of the way. Dong comes home every day to have his lunch.

Dong learns maths and Chinese at school. At breaks, his class does exercises in the playground. Dong's classroom is very plain. The school does not have much money for furniture and equipment.

Dong's classmates outside their school. They don't wear school uniforms, but everyone wears a red scarf.

Dong and his friends do exercises every day.

'I like school, but playing with my friends is more fun!' *Dong*.

Dong and his friends rush out of school at the end of the day.

Time To Play

Dong is full of energy. When he gets back from school, he rushes around the house pretending to be an aeroplane. Dong's grandmother is always telling him to be quiet. Sometimes, Dong likes to sit in the living room and read. Kung Fu books and comics are his favourites.

Xi and Xue are too young to go to school. They spend most of their time playing around the house. Sometimes, their mothers take the girls with them to the fields. Xi and Xue play together while their mothers work.

Xi and Xue play in one of the store rooms, where the family keeps baskets of rice.

Spare time

Everyone in the Wu family loves watching television.

The biggest holiday in China is the Chinese New Year. It does not have a fixed date but is usually in January or February. Families get together to eat, drink and visit relatives and friends. People decorate their houses and let off firecrackers in the streets.

After Work

The Wu family has little spare time. After a hard day's work, they all enjoy sitting down and watching television. The grown-ups like to watch the news and programmes about other places in the world.

Going To Town

The Wus don't have much money to spend on enjoying themselves. Jian Chun and Rong share a sewing machine and make their own clothes. Every now and then, they put on their best skirts and blouses and go to town. They like to look at the clothes in the shops there. Sometimes, Jian Chun and Rong go to the hairdresser for a hair cut.

Rong and Jian Chun look for bargains at the market.

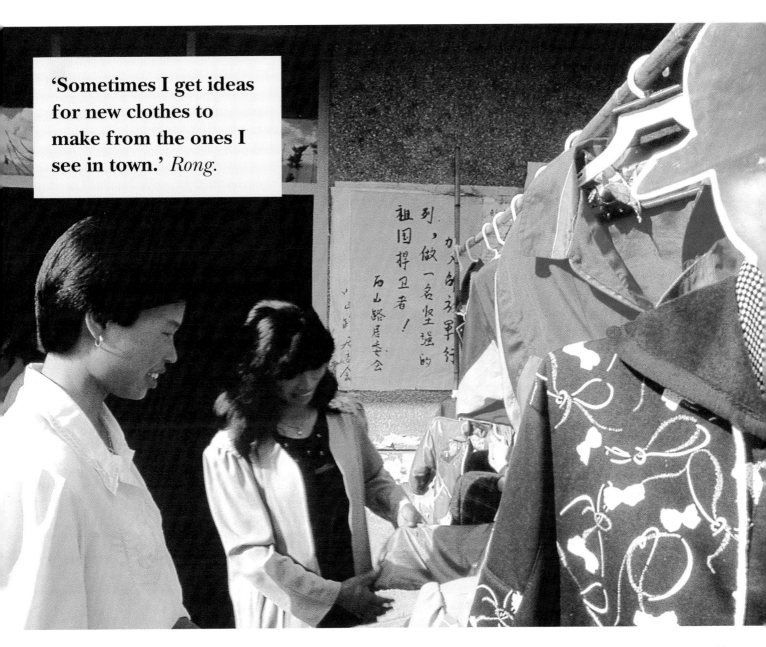

'Sometimes I get ideas for new clothes to make from the ones I see in town.' *Rong.*

The future

CHINA'S FUTURE

Life for ordinary Chinese people is better than ever before. But the population is huge and growing. In the future, one of China's big problems will be making sure that everyone has a home, and enough food, water and electricity.

The Wus are happy with their way of life. They have enough food to eat. They have been able to buy a television, radios and some new furniture. They would like a bigger television, a video-recorder and a refrigerator. Wen Bin thinks they ought to buy better tools for farming and fishing.

Dong likes playing in the fields with his sister and his friends.

28

The Wus work very hard. Every month, they are able to put some money in the bank. They are saving it to help their children as they grow up. The Wus think it is very important to look after their children's future.

Timeline

2000–221 BC	China is made up of many great kingdoms.
221 BC–AD 1911	China becomes one country, ruled by an emperor. Powerful emperors rule for hundreds of years.
1911	The last emperor is overthrown.
1949	After years of civil war, the Communists take control of China.
1949–1976	China's leader, Mao Zedong, makes great changes. Life for the poor gets much better, but there is little freedom and many people suffer.
1977	Deng Xiaoping becomes leader. China slowly opens up to the outside world. People are allowed to set up their own businesses.
1997	Deng Xiaoping dies.

Glossary

Bamboo A very strong plant with a woody stem.

Chopsticks A pair of thin sticks that Chinese people use to pick up their food.

Communists People who belong to the Communist political party. They believe that work and money should be shared out equally.

Courtyard An area surrounded by buildings or walls.

Emperor A ruler of a very large area of land.

Firecrackers Small fireworks that make a loud bang when they go off.

Fuel Materials such as wood or coal that are burned on a fire.

Kung Fu A Chinese sport.

Mosquitoes Small insects that bite. The bites are very itchy.

Noodles A dried food, made from flour. It is rather like spaghetti.

Pickle To put food in salty water or vinegar, to stop it going bad.

Population The number of people who live in a country.

Traditional Something that has been done in a certain way for a very long time.

Further information:

Books to read:

Country Insights: China by Julia Waterlow (Wayland, 1996)

C is for China by Sungwan So (Frances Lincoln, 1997)

Organizations:

Cultural Section, Chinese Embassy, 11 West Heath Road, London NW3. Tel: 0171 631 1430.

The Great Britain-China Centre, 15 Belgrave Square, London SW1X 8PS. Tel: 0171 235 6696. The Centre has a good library with information on all aspects of China, as well as slides, tapes and videos.

Index